For as long as I can remember, I have always loved to write. As a child, I loved language arts and writing stories. I remember my first diary, and I actually still have it in my possession. Writing my feelings and thoughts has never been foreign. I kept up journal writing throughout the years, and it is a favorite pastime for me as an adult. Picking out what journal I will write in excites me just the same.

I realize that not everyone journals the same and some not at all. I created this guided journal to help others partake in this pastime. Whether this is the first journal to spark your journal life or you are a long hauler like myself, it is most important to create a safe place for you to exist in.

Journaling is a time to release, to receive, and even to recreate. Journaling can take you back; it can move you forward.

It is my hope that this journal provides you a safe place to be you, that it helps you to navigate through your own waters and be free as a fish. With purpose of course.

Smiles,

About the Author

Tierra Simone Edwards was born in Charleston, South Carolina, but she calls Norcross, Georgia home where she grew up. She was born on the 2nd of March and is a true Pisces at heart! Tierra's biggest accomplishments are graduating from LeCordon Bleu with an A.S. Culinary Arts Degree and publishing her first guided journal entitled "Spoonful of Purpose". In her spare time Tierra loves to be out in nature, write, read, dance, sing , and inspire others to live like they are Born for Purpose! One of Tierra's core foundational beliefs is "Being present in every single moment granted, because every moment gives us something to take with us to our next level." The title of the guided journal was inspired by Born4Purpose Inc., whose mission is to plant seeds of purpose into the hearts of girls and women.

Tierra aspires to continue writing and publishing in the future, become a life coach for teens and young women, and establish Born4Purpose Inc as a movement that lives in the hearts of girls and women.

Tierra's love for journaling started when she received her first Hello Kitty Pink Diary with a lock on it while she was in elementary school. Her favorite subject in school by far was always language arts where she had a chance to express her creative side and write fun stories full of imagination. As Tierra got older her passion for journaling did not stop and she continued to write. Journaling became a way of life, and not just something that was done every now in then. In 2019 Tierra received a vision to create her own guided journal that was essentially reflections of her own life that she knew other women could relate to and find themselves as they began to write. The intention behind this journal is that you find you as you write.

Spoonful of Purpose Journal Guide

Atmosphere

Your surroundings are everything. Create or choose an intentional space where you will do your writing. If you will be creating a space, find a space that will be quiet and free of distractions. Place things in your space that you love, for example, candles, your favorite colors, scents, favorite pictures, plants, or a music player.

Flow

Don't think too hard! Allow yourself to release whatever comes up in your thoughts and emotions. Increase your release. Minimize the resistance.

Time

Give yourself time to write. Take your time. Treat your journal time like you would a pampering session. This is not a homework session. I encourage you to make this time a part of your life and what you do on a consistent basis. Use this time to love on you.

Journal Guide Cont.

Be You

Write like there is no tomorrow!
Write like no one will read this (because they won't). Don't be afraid of yourself.
See you.
Explore you.

Be Intentional

Make a habit of writing the date and even the time before starting each writing session. It's a gift to be able to look back and see how far you have come.

You are an evolution!

One of the greatest lessons I've learnt is how to ride the waves. I don't know if you ever watched a surfer in action or studied the sport of surfing, but if you think of the concept, it's very difficult and complex. The single fact that no wave is the same changes the game. There is always a constant learning curve in the sport of surfing. Unlike some sports, it's only there for a short period of time. I don't surf (for the record), but I have spent a lot of time observing the waves. Hearing their sounds, watching their ups and down, and witnessing their strength. And with those observations, I believe life is a lot like the sport of surfing. Everyday there is a learning curve and a new wave. And to be able to grab your surfboard, observe your wave, and ride every one is one of our greatest lessons.

"You are about to have your own personal surfing lesson as you navigate through these pages."

It is my hope that each page gives you a spoonful of purpose. Take the next few minutes to think about the waves you are currently riding in your life and write them down. As you write them down, begin to give thanks for them. All of them. No matter how small.

 *The best way to move forward in anything new is with gratitude.*

BE PRESENT.
Now

Let's put into perspective how significant your NOW is. You are planning a huge party with all the bells and whistles! There is only so much you can do in the preparation stages of the party. So much energy you can put out and tap into. You will imagine and imagine and imagine how the big day will come together...but in reality, all you have is your NOW. You will only be able to see the party in its entirety when the time comes for the celebration! But that time has to come.

Be present...Now

It's easy to believe once something happens or we finally receive something, is when we can really move forward and do what it is we have set out to do. But not everything is for later, or the future.

"Some things are for Now!"

What is in your NOW?

Spoonful of Purpose

"

Your right now is all you have. Everything else is in your imagination.
Be present!

— Tierra

Q.T.

"Where I grew up in Atlanta, Georgia we have a gas station called QT (Quick Trip). The place is literally a one-stop shop. It has everything you need, and you can fill up on gas! But this isn't about QT the gas station, instead this is about your QT (Quality Time). Your QT is similar to the gas station, it should be a one-stop shop for you to fill up on whatever you need at the moment. Similar to our cars, we need a fill up on energy, peace, clarity, strategy, encouragement, love, or just pure silence."

—Tierra

Q.T.
Personal Reflection

For today's journal time, I want you to picture yourself driving down a long road. There is only one lane on this road, and you can only go one way. It's around noon, you are the only one in the car and the only one on the road. You are riding in a beautiful orange convertible of your choice. Imagine yourself joyriding. Notice what you are wearing, down to the colors. Look ahead at the skyline. Take in the bright blue skies and the big, white, fluffy clouds. As you are driving you see a gas station up ahead. You look down at your gas level and decide it's a good time to get gas. You pull up to the pump, and you notice this pump is a little different. The gas types aren't labeled 87, 91, 93. Instead, they are labeled based on what you need in this present moment. Take a few minutes, no longer than 5 minutes, to listen to the intuition already inside of you to decide what gas you need to fill up with to continue the ride. And remember it's a one-stop shop, so go inside and grab what you may need also.

What did you fill up with? Did you go inside and grab anything else that you needed?

Spoonful of Purpose Guided Journal

Gratitude

"I imagine Gratitude a lot like a tree. A tree starts off as a seed and grows tall. It grows limbs, it sheds leaves, and seeds fall to sprout more trees. Trees produce oxygen, sap, food, housing for animals, and so much more. A lot like Gratitude. The seed is created in the heart and nourished every time you give thanks for life. Every time you are intentionally present. Anytime you give to someone else. Anytime you choose to forgive. Every time you say I love you to yourself or others. Every time you speak life. Every time you leave a tip. Every time you take in and acknowledge all that life has given you, you nurture your seeds of Gratitude."

Imagine yourself as a tree, firm with roots in the ground. You give out of abundance because your nature is to keep growing and giving. The Earth upholds you and gives you back everything you need (i.e sun, rain, birds) so you don't have to worry.

Gratitude

Gratitude is like a domino effect. Or like the gift that keeps giving. Gratitude has the ability to propel you out of your slump. When you share your gratitude with someone else, they are propelled. That moment is continuously created over and over again.

Plant seeds of gratitude today.
Display your gratitude below.

PROFIT = LOSS + LESSON

When you think about the word profit, you automatically think of a gain, an increase of some sort. But when you look at the whole picture including the mathematical equation, profit only comes after you put together and subtract what you gained from what you lost. Life is very similar. Life is full of profits even with the presence of loss. Yes, loss. Yes, loss. And loss is not limited to anything. So let's put it in context. Loss of a child, career, job, home, car, health, marriage, ANYTHING!

> *Profit only comes when we are able to be present in our moments, take, and go through the loss and gain a lesson.*

What have you profited from? Are you currently profiting from the loss of something? What lesson was attached to the loss? What loss are you currently experiencing that you can use the Profit equation to gain a new perspective on your current reality?

Momma said there'd be days like this...

You might be having, had, or will have one of the days that your mom warned you about when you were a teenager. When you thought you ruled the world. See, your mom was just trying to humble you before life got to you first. But fast forward years later, I am sure you have heard your mom's voice if not her actual voice saying, "I told you so." At this point, you may have had days where you thought you should check yourself into a mental clinic, diagnose yourself with depression, or just set yourself in time out and cry!

But a tiny fighter inside of you that you didn't know was there has stepped inside the boxing ring, because there are a lot of bets on this game, and all bets are on you!

If you are needing a journal prompt, try writing some I AM affirmations. That's always a great way to get your mind going!
I AM ......

Gentle Reminders

You are a gentle spirit. Don't push, pull, tug, or force.

Treat yourself the way you would want someone to treat you.

Give yourself space to evolve. This is not a race. You are the evolution.

Your arrivals are Godspeed.
What is meant will be and IS.
Love yourself today.
BE.

Be true to thyself!

We do not have to prove to others that the path we have chosen is the right one for us. We need only know it ourselves, but always bear in mind it is not necessarily right for others.

The beautiful thing about life is the individual mindset that we all possess. Although it is important that we use our individual mindsets as a collective for the collective, it is sometimes a process. And while that process plays out you may experience feelings of being alone, unmotivated, or even rejected. Someone may not understand your path and leave you feeling powerless, because you don't have their support. But you do have something else.

We are about to tap into your power.

What does your path entail? If you have never thought about it, take a few moments to begin envisioning it. Write what you see!

SPOONFUL OF *Purpose*

Good job! You have just taken your path, which is your vision for your life, and written it on paper. It's always helpful to get out of your mind! Now if you are like me, you have expectations for those around you to support you on this path. And I hope you are surrounded by loads of support! But if you are not at all or find that you are not supported as much as you'd like to be...that's where you come into play! Yes you!

We are going to recreate in our minds the support we want to get from others through meditation!

So you have your vision. Begin to imagine yourself walking down your path and stepping into the vision you see for yourself. So if you have a dream to open up a store, for example, begin to think about your grand opening day. You are there, of course, along with your store and everyone you want to be there. At the grand opening of your store you may want the presence of certain people. You may want for them to come up and hug you, and verbally congratulate you, amongst other things. Visualize how you want it, and let the vision play out in your mind.

The key to this meditation is envisioning the support you want down to the very detail of who, when, and how.

(Don't forget about the things you may want to hear come from that special person's mouth)

With this meditation you are consciously giving yourself the support you desire from others by tapping into your subconscious mind and your deepest desires. And manifesting at the same time! Don't underestimate the power that is your thoughts! They say a man is his thoughts!

Turn on some meditation music; get into a space where it is just you. Set the atmosphere the way you want to! Imagine. Write what you see. And allow your visions to fill you up with what you need.

Pre-Existing Conditions

Part of my self-discovery journey was signing up for inner child and shadow workshops. Those workshops really allowed for me to see my wounds and triggers for what they were and how they showed up in my life. I had some pre-existing conditions that were causing the same results in my life. Creating chaos sometimes, blockages, being stuck, or running into the same brick wall over and over again.

> *"Once I got clear of the root of these pre-existing conditions, I was able to diagnose certain things that were coming up in my life, look for, and apply a remedy. Diving deep and going within was the key!"*

Here are some questions to ask yourself to find out if you may have pre-existing conditions that need taking a deeper look into:

- *Do you find yourself always blaming someone else for your emotional state of being or the state of your life?*
- *Do you constantly need validation to feel ok or good about yourself?*
- *Is it hard for you to receive things, but you are always giving to others?*
- *Do you tend to put everyone else's needs before your own?*
- *Do you constantly feel like you need to be in control?*
- *Do you have a hard time setting boundaries, speaking up for yourself, and/or stating what you want/need?*
- *Does everything have to be perfect all the time?*
-

I have only listed a few above, so feel free to use the pages that follow to explore them or create your own!

Spoonful of Purpose Guided Journal

Your purpose requires you to be present, not perfect!

— Tierra

Spoonful of Purpose Guided Journal

SPOONFUL OF PURPOSE

LIVE ~~LOSE~~ LEARN

· DAILY REMINDER · DAILY REMINDER ·

"There's no other life to live but yours and no other purpose to pursue but the one for you!"

Ways to Elevate

● Be Present and Mindful
Bring awareness to your thoughts, emotions, and actions at all times

● Look for and submerge yourself in locations of peace
That creates a positive change in you and puts you closer to where you want to be

● Find a community that represents who you want to be

● Seek more knowledge
Learning helps you gain new perspectives and thought patterns

GENTLE REMINDERS

The Universe's language is abundance. The Universe can only meet you with abundance.

Release Affirmations

I release my learned belief that I don't live in abundance

I release my belief that I was not created out of abundance

I release myself to go bravely
I release myself to travel lightly

Reverse Energy Affirmations

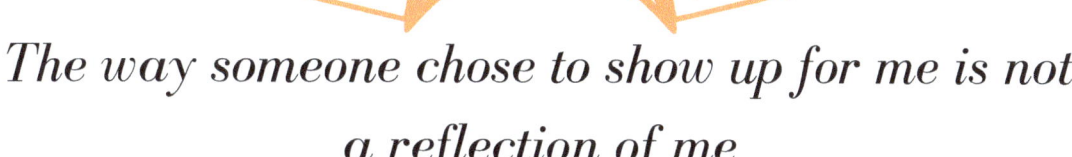

The way someone chose to show up for me is not a reflection of me

I release ownership of any guilt or shame I have taken on from someone else's actions

I cut any soul, spiritual, or emotional ties that may be using my energy without my permission

My energy will only be used as and when I see fit

I am in control of my energy

It is ok here
I am ok here
I am safe

My peace comes from within and not the ability to control everything around me

My roots run deep and cannot be uprooted

GROUNDING AFFIRMATIONS

Lost Luggage

I bumped into a lady in the store once, and she began to tell me about all her problems that she was currently having; the only thing is none of the problems she mentioned were really hers. She had absorbed those stressors from someone else. She had received those problems from someone else.

It dawned on me that there are times when we take on things that were given to us, but those things aren't ours. Nonetheless, we will carry those things with us day to day, and those things become a part of our identity.

We must give those things back, heal, and live beyond existing. Go beyond.

I am overflowing in abundance
I have everything I need right now
I deserve everything I desire
I have what is required
To fail 100x is to learn 100 lessons
I will leave nothing on the table
I love my spirit
I love my light
I love my heart

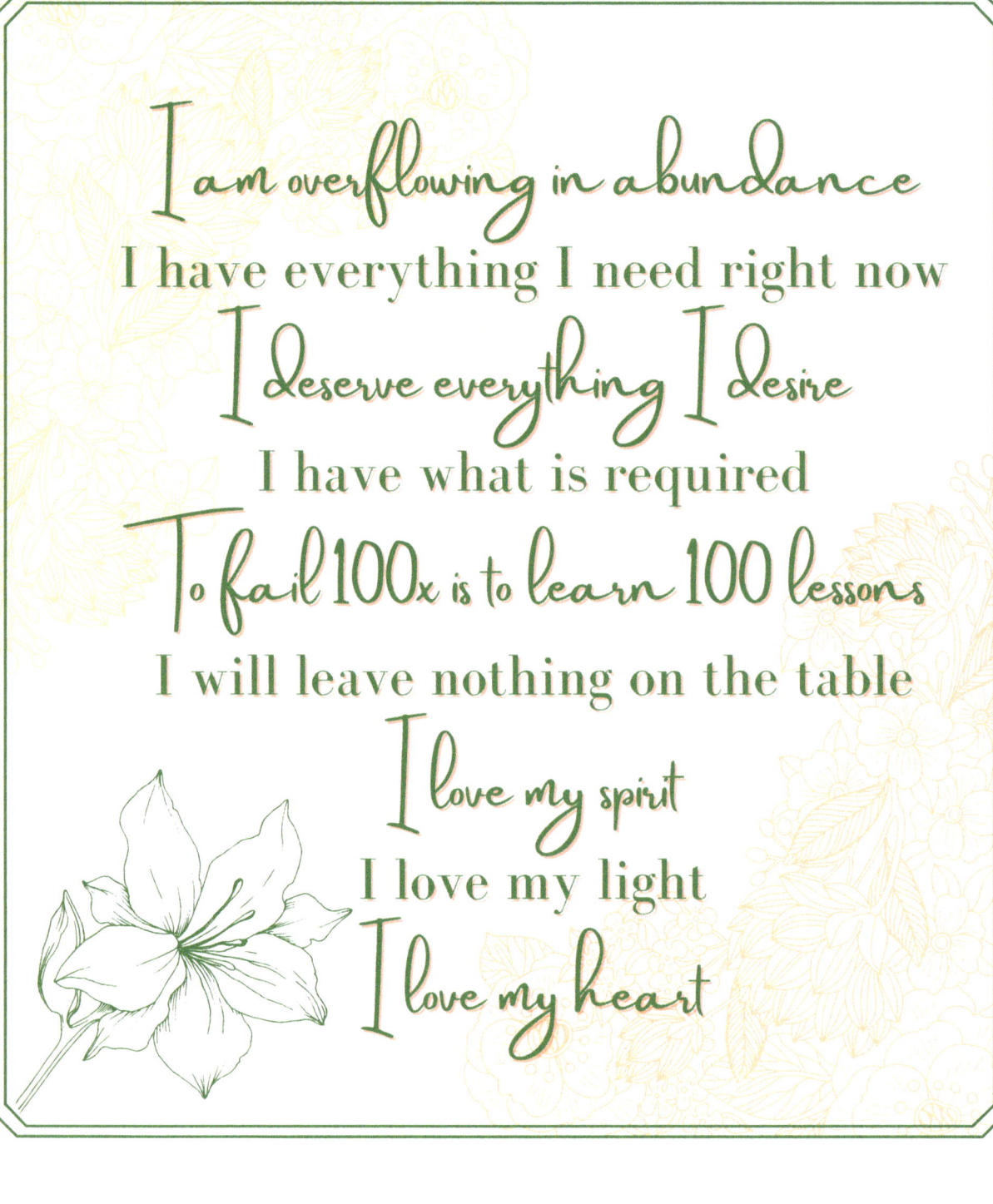

Spoonful of Purpose: Guided Journal

I receive everything good into my life and deflect everything bad.
I receive the discernment to be able to move in this world.

LET THERE BE
Light

Sometimes it's hard to see the big picture

The real reason why we are all here

The God of the universe

The love in another's eyes

The good in all mankind

The remorse in a apology

The desire to go on after the betrayal

The strength in yourself to do what's right

...or the turning point when things change.

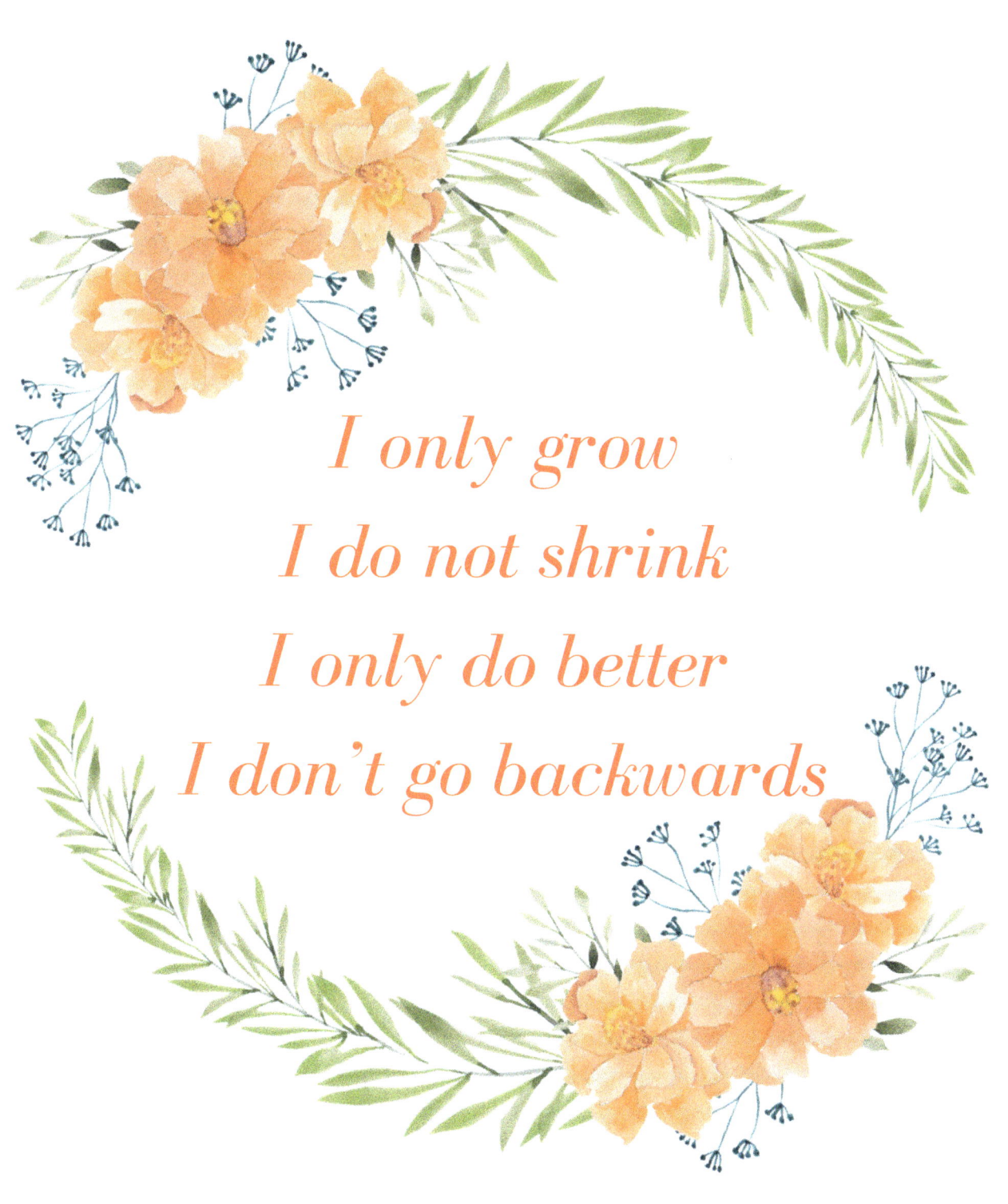

Spoonful of Purpose Guided Journal

Gentle Reminder

One morning I awoke and prepared for an online video interview. As I prepared myself, I started practicing in the mirror what I would say, how I would say it, and how I would look while I said it. A light bulb went off right at that moment. I realized I did not need to practice being me! I did not need to prepare! So I stopped what I was doing and decided to just show up as me.

You don't have to practice or prepare when you are just being YOU!
-Tierra

How does it feel when you are just being you?

Spoonful of Purpose Guided Journal

Through awareness, you can gain clarity. Through clarity, you can establish your identity. And with the knowledge of your identity, you can control your perception.

- Tierra

Spoonful of Purpose Guided Journal

SPOONFUL OF *Purpose*

We only see because of the ray of light that reflects off our eyes. And we only form a thought because of the things that we see that bounce off our experience and life. We create perception. Everything you see is a reflection.

What reflections do you see?
What reflections do you want to create?
What is your reflection?

Inner Child

Have you ever sat with the little girl inside of you? Have you ever invited her to come and sit by you? I had my first inner child experience a year ago and it was very transformative.

> ***When you get a moment, get a picture of you as a child. Sit with the picture and just look at it. Some thoughts and feelings may come up automatically. If they do that is great! Let them come. After sitting with the picture for a while, make sure that you have two seat placements. One for you and one for your little one.***

I want to invite you to have a conversation with your little one. Whoever needs to start the conversation can start, your little one may want to (☺). This is a subconscious exercise. It may feel very unfamiliar if you have never done this, but your inner child is you essentially. Your ego, your subconscious mind. Your deepest inner thoughts are your inner child as well. It is helpful for you to be in a space where you are alone, uninterrupted, and can speak aloud.

Once you have gotten settled, determine which seat is yours. If you start, you will sit in the chair that is yours and begin to talk to your little one. Get out of your head and into your heart; just flow in this moment. Say hi, ask her how she is doing, and what she may want to talk about. When it is her turn to speak you will switch seats and she will begin to talk (yes the words will still come out of your mouth; remember this is a subconscious mind exercise).

Inner Child Work

This moment is created for you to get to know yourself and your inner child more, as well as discover, revisit, or begin to heal past wounds. This helps you identify triggers and learn how to self-soothe (this is helpful in operating with other human beings).

Let this moment go for as long as it needs to.

From completing this exercise, I can now identify when my inner child is present and when I am triggered (i.e. when my inner child is having a moment). I have also learned to see potentially problematic moments a little differently, because I understand my hardwiring.

Once you introduce the woman (you) to your little one (you), they will never part. She will become your new best friend.

Use the next few pages to write about your inner child experience.

Spoonful of Purpose Guided Journal

Do you Remember?

Did you know your pain was not given to you for destruction
To close up your heart and let your spirit die
Or for your perspective on life to change
that you'd forever be blind?

Your pain was given to make strength
To help you be rooted in faith
To learn how to move through opposition
To keep your heart open so you evolve

Love through the creator is what brought you here
And love from the creator is what will keep you here
Creation is a biproduct of love
Evolution only occurs through the constant procreation
of love and creation
Remember to always remain in love
And remember the one who gave it.

Spoonful of Purpose Guided Journal

Morning Check in

- Before you get out of bed, recognize how you feel.

- Decide how you want to feel.

- While you are getting ready or if you have more time to sit, meditate on how you can arrive at your desired feeling. What actions can YOU take based on your needs?

- Have a great day!

Midday Check-in

How are you feeling?
(energetic, so-so, burnout)

What do I need? What can I do for myself? What do I need from someone else?
(based on question #1)

Release what is ineffective in this moment.
(you can write it down, say it out aloud, or write it on a sheet of paper and burn it)

Receive what you need.
(i.e. Say "I Receive" affirmations. Be ok with the outside help you asked for in #2)

Enjoy the rest of your day!

Nightly Check-in

How am I feeling?
(energetic, so-so, burnout)

What happened today that contributes to these feelings?
(based on question #1)

Is there anything that needs to be acknowledged outside of me?
(Often we silence our voice out of fear, insecurity, or not knowing how to show up for ourselves and be heard)

What can I do by the end of the night for myself that ensures I get a proper rest?

Rest Well!

Worthy Affirmations

Your worthiness is not determined by someone's inability to pay your value

Your worthiness is determined by that which you already are

Your worthiness is not determined by someone's inability to show up for you

You were created worthy!

Spoonful of Purpose Guided Journal

Gentle Reminders

I AM strength
I AM love
I AM life
I AM intentional
I AM creative
I AM light
I AM everything I need to be
I AM where I am supposed to be
The universe is my playground!
I WILL RUN!

Spoonful of Purpose Guided Journal

Acceptance

Acceptance plays a huge part in our lives, especially our experiences. You ever stop to think why recovery programs have the person admit and accept why they are there? The act of acceptance creates a flow in our lives. Therefore, the continuous act of acceptance creates a continuous flow in our lives. And that spells PROGRESS to me! The more acceptance we allow into our lives, the more flow is created. The more fulfilled we are, and the less stuck we become.

After reading the previous page, did anything pop in your mind?
If so, what ?

SELF PERFORMANCE *Review*

Typically, when you think of a performance review you think about performance reviews from others (i.e. your job.) The truth of the matter is we get performance reviews from many places: work, family, friends, significant others, etc.

And those reviews usually dictate who we are and how we operate in life.

I want us to take a different look at performance reviews. I will first start off by saying there is no other way to be except being you. And that starts from the inside out. Not just listening to other people's performance reviews of yourself, but giving yourself a performance review and knowing yourself from the inside and out.

Take charge of your own life!
Give yourself a performance review.
Allow that to be the standard for your life!

> In this section, you will find seven journal prompts to help you complete a self performance review. Take your time and reflect with purpose as you evaluate and create the standard for your life.

What accomplishments am I most proud of?

What are my goals for the next 6 months to 1 year?

Promise Affirmation

I promise to show up for me,
Allow me to be seen,
Allow me to be heard,
To nurture me,
Make me feel safe
(create a safe place),
To not leave,
Let me feel,
Ground me

What have I done to help myself have a better life? What have I done to hinder myself from having a better life?

Do I have the resources and tools I need to live life?

Instead of looking for the good or bad in every experience, look for a beneficial takeaway.

What do I want my next position in life to look like?

Are there any other concerns I have about moving forward?

In what areas would I like to evolve?

*You are not lost.
The path intended for
you brought you here.
On this path lies purpose.
Release the fear that
tries to make you resist
this journey.*

*You are not lost.
This is your path
created for you.*
Walk.

GROUNDING AFFIRMATIONS

Spoonful of Purpose Guided Journal

This portion of the journal is for you to continue showing up for yourself. Although there are no journal guiding prompts in this section, I believe if you have made it this far that you know what it looks like and how it feels to show up for you in writing. There is plenty of space beyond this point. It is my hope that as you write, you release, and as you release you heal. Take up space, sis!

— Tierra

Read to Learn, Write to Remember.

Copyright © 2021 Tierra Edwards

ISBN- 978-1-7371987-6-5
ISBN: 978-1-7371987-7-2

For information about custom editions, special sales, premium and bulk purchases, please contact:
Rackhouse Publishing Inc.
904-530-4254

First Edition
Printed in the U.S.A

www.ingramcontent.com/pod-product-compliance
Lightning Source LLC
Chambersburg PA
CBHW051331110526
44590CB00032B/4475